55 Of The Most Beautiful
Classical Piano
Solos

Masterpieces of Music

Contents

Solfeggio in D Major

Johann Christoph Friedrich Bach

March in D Major (BWV Anh. 122)

from the notebook for Anna Magdalena Bach

Johann Sebastian Bach

March in G Major (BWV Anh. 124)

from the notebook for Anna Magdalena Bach

Johann Sebastian Bach

Invention no. 4 in D Minor (BWV 775)

from the notebook for Anna Magdalena Bach

Johann Sebastian Bach

Invention no. 8 in F Major (BWV 779)

Johann Sebastian Bach

Invention no. 13 in A Minor (BWV 784)

Johann Sebastian Bach

Minuet in G Major (BWV 116)

from the notebook for Anna Magdalena Bach

Johann Sebastian Bach

Polonaise in G Minor (BWV Anh. 119)

Johann Sebastian Bach

Praeabmulum 1 in C Major (BWV 924)

Johann Sebastian Bach

Prelude in C Minor (BWV 999)

Johann Sebastian Bach

With movement

Prelude in C Major (BWV 846)

Andante

Johann Sebastian Bach

Musette in D Major (BWV Anh. 126)

from the notebook for Anna Magdalena Bach

Johann Sebastian Bach

For Elise A Minor (WoO.59)

Bagatelle No. 25

Ludwig van Beethoven

Sonate in G Major (Op.49, No.20)

Ludwig van Beethoven

Sonatina in F Major (Anh. 5, No.2)

Allegro assai

Ludwig van Beethoven

Rondo

Sonatina in G Major (Anh. 5, No.1)

Ludwig van Beethoven

Moderato

42

Arabesque (Op.100, No.2)

Johann Friedrich Burgmuller

Tarantella (Op.100, No.20)

Johann Friedrich Burgmuller

Allegro vivo

Ballade (Op.100, No.15)

Allegro con brio

Johann Friedrich Burgmuller

Polonaise in G Minor (B1)

Allegro ma non troppo

Frederic Chopin

fine

d.c. al fine

Prelude in E Minor (Op.28, No.4)

Frederic Chopin

Prelude in D-flat Major (Op.28, No.15)

Frederic Chopin

Poco più animato

Prelude in B Minor (Op.28, No.6)

Frederic Chopin

Sonatina 1 in C Major (Op.36, No.1)

Muzio Clementi

Andante

The Little Nigar (Op.28, No.6)

Claude Debussy

Arietta (Op.12, No.1)

Poco Andante e sostenuto

Edvard Grieg

Norwegian Melody (Op.12, No.6)

Edvard Grieg

Chaconne from Suite in D Minor (HWV 448, No.23)

George Frideric Handel

Variation II

Variation III

Variation IV

Variation V

Variation VI

Variation VII

74

Suite in D Minor (HWV 437)

George Frideric Handel

Allmande

Courante

Sarabande

Variation I

Variation II

Gigue

81

Minuet in F Major

Franz Joseph Haydn

Variations on an Austrian Folk Song (Op.42, No.1)

Friedrich Kuhlau

Variation 2

Variation 3

Variation 4

Variation 5

Variation 6

Songs Without Words (Op.30, No.3)

Felix Mendelssohn Bartholdy

cre - scen - - do

Songs Without Words (Op.19, No.6)

Venetian Gondola Song

Felix Mendelssohn Bartholdy

Songs Without Words (Op.30, No.6)

Venetian Gondola Song

Felix Mendelssohn Bartholdy

Allegro in B-Flat Major (K.3)

for Pianoforte

Wolfgang Amadeus Mozart

Minuet in C Major (K.6)

For Piano

Wolfgang Amadeus Mozart

Andante

Minuet 1.)

Minuet 2.)

Minuet in F Major (K.2)

Wolfgang Amadeus Mozart

Minuet in F Major (K.5)

Wolfgang Amadeus Mozart

Minuet in G Major (K.1)

for Piano

Wolfgang Amadeus Mozart

Menuetto da Capo al Fine

Piano Sonata No.11 in A Major (K.331/3)

"Alla Turca"

Wolfgang Amadeus Mozart

Var. 6   Allegro

Sonate in C Major (K.545)

Allegro

Wolfgang Amadeus Mozart

Fugue in A Minor (P 162)

Johann Pachelbel

Minuet in G Major (BWV Anh.114)

Christian Petzold

Gymnopedie No.1

Eric Satie

Scenes from Childhood (Op.15, No.4)

Robert Alexander Schumann

First Loss (Op.68, No.16)

Robert Alexander Schumann

Siciliana (Op.68, No.11)

Album for the Young

Robert Alexander Schumann

*(Comme au début et sans
répétitions jusqu'à la fin.)*

(Fin.)

Scenes from Childhood 7 (Op.15, No.7)

7. Reverie

Robert Alexander Schumann

The Wild Horseman (Op.68, No.8)

Robert Alexander Schumann

Gigue in G Major

Georg Philipp Telemann

The Sick Doll (Op.39, No.7)

Pyotr Ilyich Tchaikovsky

Old French Song (Op.39, No.16)

Andantino

Pyotr Ilyich Tchaikovsky

The Doll's Funeral (Op.39, No.7)

Pyotr Ilyich Tchaikovsky

The New Doll (Op.39, No.6)

Italian Song (Op.39, No.15)

Pyotr Ilyich Tchaikovsky

Moderato

Made in the USA
Columbia, SC
03 July 2020